BULLYING
AND
SEXUAL HARASSMENT

Tina Stephens is a principal lecturer with the Wrexham Business School at the North East Wales Institute of Higher Education. She is also the IPD's national examiner for management processes and functions, and managing activities. As an academic she lectures and writes on a wide range of human resource management issues. A mixture of roles as a personnel professional and line manager has made her only too aware of the challenges that the day-to-day management of people presents. She delivers seminars and workshops on various aspects of managerial behaviour, and is particularly keen to blend research and theory with a practical, down-to-earth approach designed to help those at the 'sharp end'.

The Institute of Personnel and Development is the leading publisher
of books and reports for personnel and training professionals,
students, and all those concerned with the effective management
and development of people at work. For details of all our titles,
please contact the Publishing Department:

tel 020 8263 3387

fax 020 8263 3850

e-mail publish@ipd.co.uk

The catalogue of all IPD titles can be viewed on the IPD website:

www.ipd.co.uk

BULLYING AND SEXUAL HARASSMENT

TINA STEPHENS

INSTITUTE OF PERSONNEL AND DEVELOPMENT

Design and typesetting by
Wyvern 21, Bristol

Printed in Great Britain by
the Short Run Press, Exeter

British Library Cataloguing in Publication Data
A catalogue record for this book is available
from the British Library

ISBN 0-85292-825-4

NB Throughout this publication the male gender has,
in general, been used for convenience, but it should
be read to include the female gender

INSTITUTE OF PERSONNEL
AND DEVELOPMENT

IPD House, Camp Road, Wimbledon, London SW19 4UX
Tel.: 020 8971 9000   Fax: 020 8263 3333
Registered office as above. Registered Charity No. 1038333
A company limited by guarantee. Registered in England No. 2931892

Contents

Other titles in the series

What is harassment?

The dictionary tells us that to harass is 'to annoy often or to make sudden attacks on'. This seems quite apt when related to harassment in the workplace, but definitions and examples of what constitutes such behaviour are many and varied. The guiding principles are that the behaviour is both unwelcome and persistent. Harassment may involve individuals or groups of individuals and, in terms of the traditional organisational hierarchy, it is no respecter of status. The manager (boss) may bully the subordinate, the subordinate may harass the boss, and colleagues may bully or harass each other individually or in groups. Even when symptoms become obvious the difficulty lies in unearthing the causes and eradicating them.

The IPD's statement on Harassment at Work (now the Key Fact Sheet on Harassment at Work) reminds us that people can be subject to harassment for many reasons, including their:

- race, ethnic origin, nationality or skin colour
- gender or sexual orientation
- age or youth
- religious or political convictions
- inability or unwillingness to assert themselves.

This guide deals with the two forms of harassment that are most prevalent in all workplaces: bullying and sexual harassment. As acts of harassment, they have much in common; the victims are very vulnerable and often reluctant to complain, particularly as they may fear reprisals. Usually they just want the behaviour to stop.

Harassment is not a new phenomenon but it is receiving much greater attention because of an increasingly diverse workforce and changing attitudes to equal opportunities and to what is acceptable behaviour at work.

The signs and symptoms of harassment are many and varied; illness, absenteeism, poor performance or resigning from the job are the most obvious. These signs and symptoms will have an effect on the lives of individuals at work and at home. They include:

	Impact at work	Impact at home
Fear	✓	✓
Stress	✓	✓
Anxiety	✓	✓
Illness	✓	✓
Absenteeism	✓	
Apparent lack of commitment	✓	
Poor performance	✓	
Resigning from the job	✓	✓
Conflict	✓	
Poor morale	✓	✓
High labour turnover	✓	
Reduced productivity	✓	
Low efficiency	✓	
Accidents	✓	✓
Reduced quality	✓	
Divided teams	✓	

This list shows the major impact areas though, of course, problems at work are always likely to have some impact on home life eventually.

Harassment may be present in the form of:

violence	setting unattainable targets at work
deliberately ignoring someone	posters
jokes	graffiti
offensive language	obscene gestures
gossip	coercion for sexual favours
slander	pestering
sectarian songs, letters or rhymes	spying
sarcasm	stalking
unfounded criticism	

Cases of harassment that reach the public eye through the media are usually those where a tribunal case or national survey has elicited the revelation of graphic, sometimes sensationalised, detail. These, however, are only a very small tip of a very large iceberg. Organisations that conduct their own workplace harassment surveys are few and are usually shocked by what they discover.

Bullying is not always a sudden burst of temper resulting in a one-off instance of verbal or physical abuse. It is persistent and frequently includes the misuse of power gained from the bully's status in the organisation. It may be hidden from public view, though more often it would seem to involve acts of public humiliation.

Tim Field describes bullying as a form of violence: 'It's aggression expressed psychologically rather than physically – it's harmful. It can be more devastating than a physical injury and is compounded by denial and unenlightenedness.' (*Bully in Sight*, T. Field 1996).

A bully is someone who unfairly uses his or her size and strength to hurt or frighten weaker persons. That size and strength does not of course have to be physical. Status and power in the work environment can amount to the same thing. The focus for bullying is actually rarely based on gender, race or disability: it is more likely to feature the competence, or rather the alleged incompetence, of the victim. It can be typified in this example from the TUC Survey on Workplace Bullying:

> My ex-boss used to manage his staff by humiliation. He would make people who did not reach the impossible targets he set stand in the corner wearing a dunce's hat . . . Staff were terrified – some of them literally jumped every time he walked into the room.

Sexual harassment may take many forms: it can be verbal, non-verbal or physical. Examples include unsolicited sexual advances and propositions, lewd comments and innuendo, pornographic or sexually suggestive pictures or written materials, and physical contact with another employee.

It is well known that many people meet their future partner at work and indeed that intimate relationships, proper and improper, can flourish in the works canteen, at the drinks dispenser or in the store cupboard. It is only when such behaviour is unsolicited and unwelcome that it becomes sexual harassment. This in itself can cause a dilemma because victims often do not come forward, and even if they do, the harasser may declare lack of intention. 'Just being friendly', 'Only a bit of a laugh' are common protestations and denials.

Though there have been cases where one incident has been sufficiently serious to warrant a justifiable complaint, sexual attention usually becomes classified as harassment if it persists and it has been made clear that it is regarded by the recipient as offensive and unwanted. As with bullying, the behaviour may be hidden and secretive, but it may instead be public, with the result that it embarrasses and humiliates the victim even more. Workplace harassment can be combated and resolved not only by developing and implementing preventive policies and procedures but also by ensuring an organisational culture and management style that fosters openness, trust and support.

Organisations conducting anonymous attitude surveys may be surprised to find significant allegations of bullying or sexual harassment and will need to be prepared to deal with them! Employers who receive few or no complaints about harassment should not be complacent. Remember, one crucial dilemma for the victim in these circumstances is whether or not to blow the whistle for fear of reprisal and further victimisation, The individual may be very reluctant to come forward even to get the unwanted behaviour stopped. Even then, the spectre of involvement in subsequent investigations, disciplinary and even legal proceedings may be too daunting for many employees, who really just want to get on with their jobs and their lives.

So it's your problem now! You need to discover the size of that problem and begin to tackle it now!

As a personnel professional, you have several important responsibilities including contributing to the success of your organisation in achieving its business objectives and maintaining the dignity and quality of working life for the people it employs. These responsibilities must be taken seriously. The short-term and long-term implications of missing or under-performing members of the workforce are crucial to the business.

It is your challenge to raise awareness and facilitate any changes that need to be made.

Why should I do anything about it?

☑ You could be breaking the law
☑ What will bullying and sexual harassment cost the organisation?
  Potential direct cost – Potential indirect cost

You could be breaking the law

Legislation and quasi-legislation (eg codes of practice) relating to bullying and sexual harassment is by no means comprehensive and for some cases it seems there is no recourse to the law. As with much of our employment legislation, we find a mixture originating from both Brussels and Westminster, with the obvious need for statute to be added to and further defined by case law. What is important for both employer and employee to recognise, however, is that there are penalties that can be imposed and that compensation can be awarded.

The main relevant sources of law are:

- Sex Discrimination Act (1975)
- Protection from Harassment Act (1996)
- Employment Rights Act (1996)
- Public Interest Disclosure Act (1998)
- EC Council Directive 26/207 (Equal Treatment)
- EC Recommendation and Code of Practice on Protecting the Dignity of Men and Women at Work (1991).

In addition to this, cases have been fought successfully under the Criminal Justice and Public Order Act (1994) and through claims for personal injury and breach of contract.

A brief review reveals the following important and useful information:

> It is unlawful for a person, in the case of a woman employed by him at an establishment in Great Britain, to discriminate against her by dismissing her or subjecting her to any other detriment.

The Manager's responsibility under the Sex Discrimination Act 1975, s41, is described thus:

> Anything done by a person in the course of his employment shall be treated as done by his employer as well as by him, whether it was done with or without the employer's knowledge or approval.

Two famous cases have further illustrated the employer's responsibility:

Jones v *Tower Boot Co. Ltd* (1997)

the employer is responsible for acts of employees within the workplace, unless the actions clearly go beyond the employer's control

and

Burton v *De Vere Hotels* (1996)

the employer is directly liable for harassment which he could control. Complaints of harassment must be taken seriously by managers, who must undertake a thorough investigation – otherwise, they may be in fundamental breach of contract.

The EC Recommendation and Code of Practice on Protecting the Dignity of Men and Women at Work is not legally binding 'but should be taken into account by national courts'. Article One refers to conduct which is 'unwanted, unreasonable and offensive to the recipient' and which 'creates an intimidating, hostile or humiliating work environment for the recipient'. Article Two requires member states to 'create a climate at work in which men and women respect one another's dignity'.

Statutory provision is now available against dismissal and victimisation for any employee who speaks out against wrongdoing in the workplace, provided that certain conditions are met (Public Disclosure Act, 1998). While most of the instances involve the disclosure of confidential information, bullying and harassment practices which may have become institutionalised through the culture can still be included. *For protection, the disclosure must consist of information which tends to show one or more of the following:*

- a criminal offence
- failure to comply with a legal obligation
- miscarriage of justice
- danger to the health and safety of an individual
- damage to the environment
- the deliberate concealment of information.

> The employee is protected if a qualifying disclosure is made in good faith to his/her employer or to another person when the employee reasonably believes the failure relates solely or mainly to the conduct of that person or to a matter for which that person has legal responsibility.
>
> Section 43c, Public Disclosure Act

The law also suggests that the employee can go to 'prescribed persons' such as health and safety representatives or the Health and Safety Executive.

Protection against dismissal and/or victimisation exists if:

- the employee makes the disclosure in good faith
- the employee believes that the disclosure is substantially true
- there is no personal gain for the employee
- the employee believes that he or she will be subjected to detriment by the employer if the disclosure is made
- there is no one in the organisation to tell
- the complaint has already been made and nothing has been done.

So can it be taken out of my hands?

An employer *must* investigate complaints. Failure to deal with a complaint may amount to a breach of trust and confidence, and therefore neglect of the employer's duty of care, as the following case illustrates (*Hatrick* v *City Fax*, OIT 3041/138).

An employee [Ms Hatrick] had her hair forcibly cut by a colleague. She was distressed and reported the incident to the personnel manager. Management decided to take no action over what they considered to be a minor act of stupidity because it might escalate the situation. The tribunal thought that employees were entitled to expect protection from this sort of behaviour.

Any reasonable employee would have had her confidence shaken if her employer had decided to take no action when faced with 'a blatant case of horseplay or bullying', and a reasonable employer would have responded immediately to the complaint.

Both quotations are from EAT.

The employer's failure to act was a fundamental breach of contract entitling Ms Hatrick to resign and claim constructive dismissal.

The Code of Practice on Protecting the Dignity of Women and Men at Work (1991) describes sexual harassment as 'unwanted conduct of a sexual nature, or other conduct based on sex, affecting the dignity of men and women at work' General harassment includes 'situations where a person's rejection of, or submission to, such conduct on the part of employers or workers is used explicitly or implicitly as a basis for a decision which affects a person's employment prospects'.

There could be huge costs to the organisation.

What will bullying and sexual harassment cost the organisation?

Potential direct cost

Bullying and sexual harassment is happening in your organisation now. Independent surveys show that around one in five UK employees falls victim. The number of employees feeling secure at work fell from 76 per cent in 1990 to 43 per cent in 1997. High morale has declined from 52 per cent to 39 per cent in the same period (Research Group ISR January 1997).

- Thirty-five per cent of British managers feel insecure at work, as do 59 per cent of junior and middle managers (Employment Policy Institute, November 1996).
- Estimates of the cost of stress and stress-related illness range from £5 billion (TUC) to £12 billion (CBI) each year.
- £500 for each working adult!
- On average, sickness absence costs employers £485 per year per employee (HSE).
- Six million working days are lost each year because of stress – the main causes being bullying and harassment, job insecurity, shift work and long hours.

- Replacing employees on a temporary or permanent basis averages out at over £500 per head including recruitment, training and settling -in costs.
- Grievance procedures cost on average £1,000 in staff time for each stage.
- Employment tribunals cost on average £10,000 +.
- Employment tribunals' proceedings may last from several days to several years.
- County Court actions cost on average £50,000 +.
- High Court actions cost on average £100,000 +.
- Appeals to the House of Lords cost on average £100,000 + and take three years.
- Cases referred to European Courts cost on average over £1 million and take five years.

Your organisation certainly doesn't want to make this kind of financial commitment! If bullying and sexual harassment exist and are allowed to continue, then that is exactly what it could be doing.

Potential indirect cost

For the organisation, bullying and sexual harassment may lead to:

- increased absenteeism
- increased overtime
- reduction in quality standards
- missed deadlines
- poor customer service
- reduced employee morale
- increased labour turnover
- reduced customer satisfaction
- increasing number of accidents

13

- increased need for closer supervision
- poor decision-making or a lengthening of the process.

For the individual, suffering bullying and sexual harassment directly may lead to:

- loss of career
- loss of livelihood
- loss of confidence
- separation and divorce
- depression and even suicide.

For the individual who is not suffering directly from bullying and sexual harassment there is still a cost:

- extra work to cover for absent or under-performing colleagues
- inability to carry out his or her own job because of under-performance or mistakes by others
- accidents caused by others
- loss of bonus.

These eventually lead to his or her own stress. The effect can be like falling dominoes. The Health and Safety Executive estimates that for 1994 the cost of stress and stress-related illness to industry and the tax payers was £4 billion per year. In 1997 the cost was £12 billion (CBI).

Spend £5,000 a year on anti-harassment training. Just avoiding one serious case makes this a cost-effective arrangement.

Bank of England: bullying

The bank recognises that all staff have the right to be treated with dignity and respect, and encourages staff to behave in such a manner towards each other.

Bullying is harmful. It causes distress and can lead to accidents, illness and poor performance. Bullying is defined as any unsolicited or unwelcome act that humiliates, intimidates or undermines the individual involved. No form of bullying will be condoned at work or outside work if it has a bearing on the working relationship.

Reproduced from 'Bullying at work: a survey of 157 employers', in *IRS Employee Health Bulletin*, April 1999.

What can I do about it?

Establishing a policy

One policy or several?

Any instance of sexual harassment or bullying will be easier
to resolve if the organisation has an established policy and
procedures for dealing with it.

Many organisations already have such mechanisms in
place for issues of sexual harassment and use these to deal
with bullying. In other instances equal opportunities or
even grievance policy and procedures are used.

Policies used to deal with bullying

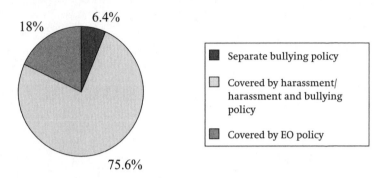

18% 6.4%

75.6%

■ Separate bullying policy

□ Covered by harassment/ harassment and bullying policy

■ Covered by EO policy

IRS survey into bullying at work, April 1999

Is our existing equal opportunities policy enough?

Where a policy for sexual harassment or equal opportunities is 'broadened' to include bullying, the name is often changed. For example, it becomes a policy for 'maintaining dignity at work'. Just changing the title may not be enough, and if every new area of victimisation or other wrong treatment at work is going to be another paragraph in an existing policy, it is unlikely that the effect will be positive. This 'tagging on' process is better achieved by a review of the existing policy and procedures. The new areas of behaviour need to be fully integrated. It is even suggested that a separate policy and procedures need to be established to deal with bullying.

In order of preference, you should have:

- separate policies for sexual harassment and bullying
- bullying policy incorporated into sexual harassment policy

18

- bullying and sexual harassment policies incorporated into equal opportunities policy
- bully and sexual harassment issues dealt with through grievance and disciplinary procedures.

No policy is perfect, but it will show everyone in the organisation that you are serious about the issues and that you will endeavour to:

- treat all cases fairly and quickly
- do everything possible to eradicate such types of behaviour.

What is policy?

Organisations will have policies regarding most facets of their business. They provide:

- an expression of broad intentions
- an expression of what to do in a given situation
- an expression of organisational culture.

They also serve to:

- guide attitude
- guide decisions
- guide actions.

What's the best approach to policy for my organisation? Depending on the size and nature of the organisation, the policy will fall somewhere along the following spectrum:

No policy ←→ Assumed policy ←→ Informal policy ←→ Full, formal explicit policy

The extent to which that policy is communicated will range from:

Covert	← →	Overt
known by only a few and not committed to paper		published and available to all staff

The decision about where to put your organisation on this spectrum is not all that straightforward. Too full, explicit and overt might mean less flexibility and it is unlikely that any two cases of bullying and sexual harassment will be the same. Too covert, and there is likely to be inconsistency and indecision.

However, because this issue is such a sensitive one, and in order at best to discourage such behaviour and at least to encourage victims to come forward, then a more explicit approach is recommended.

Why does policy about bullying and sexual harassment need to be explicit?
An explicit policy will:

- provide all employees with indications of probable decisions that will be made in particular circumstances
- express uniformity of intentions regarding employee demands for fairness and equity
- provide predictability for repetitive situations
- show that the management of the organisation has thought in advance how possible contingencies will be dealt with
- enable top management to influence decisions at all levels

- provide a framework within which it is easier to assess the effect of policy and, where necessary, to achieve change
- give those formulating the policy problem-solving experience
- establish the limits on decisions to be taken by individual managers
- ensure greater consistency.

How is policy made effective?

If the proper amount of time and energy is expended on putting the policy and procedures in place, then that in itself may dramatically reduce bullying and sexual-harassment-related behaviour. To be effective the policy should be:

- stated in positive terms
- in writing
- widely distributed and publicised
- applied fairly and uniformly
- related to the on-going business context
- constantly updated.

Designing and drafting your bullying and sexual harassment policy

Have you:

- consulted widely inside and outside the organisation
- got a clear statement from top management on how bullying and sexual harassment is viewed by the organisation
- established a variety of means for publicity and awareness-raising

- ensured that the procedure for dealing with complaints is confidential
- ensured that the treatment of those accused is professional and sensitive
- ensured that the procedure for dealing with complaints is quick but thorough, with a time scale for responses
- trained staff to identify actual or potential problem situations
- trained staff to counsel those involved
- considered how to deal with the aftermath for both the victim and perpetrator
- made it proactive
- ensured that written records will be kept
- made both individuals and managers responsible for their actions?

Who can help to put the right policy in place?

First, remember that yours is not the only organisation with these problems, and not the only one devising policies and procedures to deal with them. The Consumers Association (CA) introduced an anti-harassment policy in 1995 as a joint initiative between the staff bodies and human resources department. A significant survey conducted by the Manufacturing, Science and Finance Union and National Union of Journalists showed that employees felt there was a need for such a policy. The CA says 'The policy was introduced to help create an environment in which staff could work free from the threat of bullying and other forms of harassment. There were also sound business reasons for introducing the policy because we knew that the costs of dealing with conflict, absenteeism, low morale and low productivity are high.'

With Rolls Royce the policy began as one relating to sexual harassment, introduced in 1996. 'As we were developing the sexual harassment policy it became clear that we needed to combine racial harassment and bullying – three evils which can have a real impact on business efficiency.'

While there will be some organisational differences, the fundamental principles and framework are bound to be similar.

You have access to information, advice and support from several sources:

Externally:

- other employers locally or in your particular sector
- professional bodies
- trade unions
- employer organisations
- advisory services
- publications.

Internally:

- using consultative committees or perhaps establishing these for the first time to deal with this issue
- analysing the culture, structure and management style of the organisation to establish 'best fit'
- surveys.

When should I start?

Some organisations introduce their policy following cases in the workplace which may or may not have led to disciplinary action or legal proceedings. Some organisations are more proactive, following recommended best practice and learning from others' painful and expensive experiences. *Being proactive is best.*

Examining organisational culture, structure and management style

The size, structure and culture of your organisation is worth examining to highlight potential causes of harassment or failure to deal with it. Organisations exist to pursue varied objectives and may operate in different ways, but none can justify the abuse of employees through harassment in the achievement of those objectives.

Culture

This has been best defined by Charles Handy in *Understanding Organisations* as 'the way we do things around here'.

Culture must be seen as a two-way process: it shapes the behaviour of all employees and they in turn shape the way the organisation performs. Different departments or sites in the same organisation may show cultural differences, and a healthy organisation will tolerate and absorb this. Culture includes deep-set beliefs about work organisation, authority, reward and control, and an understanding of culture is essential if any change process or procedure is envisaged.

This means that what might be 'acceptable' behaviour in one department or organisation would not be tolerated in another – offensive language, for example, or the frequent playing of practical jokes. It could be said that if all employees accept the culture, then even if it is inappropriate from a 'best practice' point of view it should be allowed to continue, but evidence has shown that although people do 'accept' the culture this may be because they need the job and are too scared to speak out. Ask yourself, 'Should culture as it is, even if it is inappropriate from a best practice point of view, continue if it breaks the law and treats individuals or groups without respect and dignity, or worse still, with degradation and humiliation?' In understanding the culture of your organisation some external 'best practice' benchmarking might be the way to determine the potential or actual existence of harassment and choose the best way to deal with it.

Structure

The structure of the organisation will dictate in particular where the power lies, and it is the abuse of power that so often leads to harassment. Autocracy will place the decision-making focus in the hands of the few. In a small organisation this may well be the owner only, and the treatment of people may be at a whim and without a two-way dialogue. If the owner/manager values employees, then harassment is unlikely. If he or she does not, then there may be little that can be done. Stemming from autocracy, in the bigger organisation bureaucracy will emerge. Power will continue to be held or focused centrally and the structure will spawn its own procedures and red tape to ensure strict control of behaviour. Both of these structures emphasise the elevation of the few above the many, and restrict any communication other than top-down.

Finally, a matrix may be the focus for the organisation, with power and authority constantly shifting as projects are completed and objectives met. Here leaders or 'bosses' are in their positions based on their given skills for a fixed period of time. A manager who is soon going to be a colleague again may have a different approach to the treatment of others!

Recently the de-layering of many organisations has brought more decision-making power to different levels, and many managers act as mentors or coaches rather than as Admirals or Emperors. This in itself requires collaboration rather than confrontation, and so should induce more harmonious working relationships.

Modern organisation structures are, in the main, flatter and leaner to make them more efficient. The decision-making is nearer the coal face and nearer the customer. Individuals at work are encouraged to monitor their own work, and to make their own decisions. Project teams, drawn together from across the spectrum of the organisation, plan and organise. E-mails and intranets make communications direct and immediate. Though positive changes in many ways, these new ways of working may lead to uncertainty and conflict for managers and their staff. Managers in particular can become anxious and lose confidence as they move from telling and directing to asking and facilitating.

Management style

Management style will emerge from the structure and culture, and to be effective the three should show complementarity. With decision-making power in the hands of the few, an autocratic controlling management style will evolve, nothing being done if it doesn't please 'the boss'. No checks and balances, and top managers who are all of the same mind, will lead inevitably to the abuse of power and is a hotbed for breeding harassment.

Bureaucracy, too, could be dangerous, but this depends on what type of procedural red tape is present. It is fine if it has sound bullying and sexual harassment procedures, but not so if it really is 'bound', because all actions will be governed or even hidden by bureaucratic red tape.

A more democratic, involved, empowering style of management will make the manager (boss) much more accountable to his or her staff and much more transparent in his or her actions.

Managers may well be confused about their role and their legitimate use of 'power'. Have you reviewed their job descriptions? Have you trained them in 'new' management techniques?

Managerial behaviour is influenced by five major sources:

- senior management
- peers
- themselves and their preferred approach
- subordinates
- customers.

The design of the manager's job needs to be reviewed to reveal any conflict or confusion. Once the role is better defined with parameters for acceptable and legitimate behaviour revealed to all staff, everyone can see where a manager is overstepping the line.

What can help to accommodate culture, structure and managerial style?

- Has your organisation become leaner and flatter?
- Have your managers had recent management training?

- Do senior managers understand the legal and financial implications of bullying and sexual harassment?
- Do your managers all 'sing to the same hymn sheet' when dealing with staff in what could be seen as a fair and respectful way?
- Do your employees understand the legitimate power and authority of the boss and the wider organisation in terms of what they can rightly expect to have said and done to them at work?

Power and authority

Inevitably linked with culture and management style is the use of power and authority in the organisation. Power is often abused in bullying and sexual harassment cases. It's important that you understand what it is and how it works.

Power may come through position, expertise, control over information or over other resources. It may also embrace or control other rewards and punishments. The chief executive is powerful, and so is the chief executive's secretary!

> Power lies in the acceptance of your authority by others, their knowledge that if they try to resist you they will fail and you will succeed. Real power does not lie in documents, it lies in what you can achieve.
>
> Anthony Jay, *Management and Machiavelli*, Hemel Hempstead, Prentice Hall, 1994

It is the use of power that can determine whether the manager is simply macho or oversteps the line and becomes a bully.

> Managers must possess a high need for power, that is, a concern for influencing people. However, this need must be disciplined and controlled so that it is directed towards the benefit of the Institution as a whole and not towards the manager's personal aggrandisement.

> McClelland, *Power: The great motivator*, 1976

So the successful exercise of power requires:

- using power openly and legitimately
- being sensitive to what types of power are most effective with different people
- developing all sources of power and not relying on just one technique
- seeking jobs and tasks which will give opportunity for the use of power
- using power in a mature and self-controlled way
- deriving satisfaction from influencing others.

Communicating the policy

At the design stage

First, awareness of the organisation's policy may be raised at the time of its design (or redesign). Using an existing group, eg a consultative committee or equal opportunities group, gives an excellent opportunity to discover what employees are looking for from the policy. Either of these groups is likely to be representative of the organisational cross-section.

Use their suggestions, add your external knowledge, and return to them and senior management during the development stage. A policy that has been jointly drawn up and designed is more likely to be accepted and adhered to. By the time the policy is written and accepted its existence and content should have become well known.

Once the policy and attendant procedures have been accepted there is a danger that the papers will pass to the desk drawer of the personnel manager, into the staff handbook, and the into minutes of the working party by whom it was devised. Isn't that a good thing? Doesn't it mean that no harassment is taking place? Probably not – it just means it isn't being dealt with! The exercise has therefore been a complete waste of time.

Something as important as this needs to be flagged up as often as possible – it is surprising how such issues pass people by!

A huge flurry of excitement at its instigation is all well and good, but what about 12 months down the line? Any potential victim needs to know his or her rights but the bully or harasser may choose not to be familiar with the policy, thus claiming ignorance when involved in any investigation.

Who needs to know?

- New staff:
  - in letters of appointment
  - contracts of employment
  - induction pack and programme

- Existing staff:
  - notice boards
  - newsletter
  - cloakrooms and changing rooms

- canteen and rest rooms
- staff handbook

- Managers:
  - (as well as the general information that is available to all staff)
  - regular debriefing where bullying and harassment has occurred
  - in any department
  - regular reminders of the procedures and penalties

- Contractors/ suppliers:
  - make it part of the terms of the contract that the policy should be honoured
  - encourage them to adopt similar policies.

What information do people need?

- the procedure
- the penalties
- the confidentiality and counselling available
- names and locations of people to go to.

Consult, construct and agree a policy statement

This must show how the policy will:

- treat all cases fairly
- confidentiality
  - listening to all sides without jumping to conclusions

31

- keeping those involved aware of what progress is being made

- get rid of the behaviour
  - being proactive not reactive
  - emphasising that all cases will be thoroughly investigated
  - outlining procedure and corrective action
  - setting goals and improvement targets for dealing with the problem.

Use the policy!

Remember, this will include not only monitoring incidents but looking at the culture, structure and management style of the organisation. Are the norms acceptable? Can we use the excuse that 'this is the way we do things around here' if we are contravening legislation and damaging the dignity of people at work?

What procedures should we adopt and develop?

- ☑ Complaints procedure
- ☑ Procedures and investigation

    Informal stage – Formal stage – . . . And afterwards? –
    Checklist – How do we conduct an investigation? –
    How do we conduct the interview? – Monitoring cases
    and their outcomes – What happens next? – How does
    mediation work? – Statistical data – Financial data –
    Surveys and exit interviews

Complaints procedure

It is essential that a procedure is put into place to allow for any claims of bullying and harassment to be dealt with quickly, fairly, confidentially and objectively. All employees need ready access to that procedure without having to ask for a copy. It's a good idea to post copies, or at least the main points, in cloakrooms, dining rooms or other public places.

In addition to this, employees must be encouraged to use the procedure, and it needs to be monitored and reviewed to ensure that it is working. It must allow employees to bypass line managers or supervisors who may be the cause for complaint. Standard grievance procedures are not considered to be a suitable means of dealing with bullying and sexual harassment because of the very personal and sometimes intimate and embarrassing nature of the offence.

This is particularly the case with sexual harassment, where normally grievances would first be raised with the line manager. Very often the line manager for a woman is a man (and of course there are a growing number of instances where the boss is female and the harassment is being suffered by a male subordinate). Some women may fear they will not be taken seriously and this may dissuade them from pursuing a complaint. Men may feel that they are demonstrating a weakness if they have to discuss the issue with a female boss.

A two-stage procedure is recommended allowing for an initial informal investigation. Should that not resolve the issue then a formal procedure may be instigated. The Employment Appeal Tribunal recommends that any complaint should be dealt with 'from the perception of the person aggrieved' but it is also important that individuals are not deemed to be guilty until proved innocent.

Finally, some recommendations must be made clear with regard to what happens after decisions have been reached.

Procedures and investigation

Informal stage

Here the individual should be given the opportunity to discuss the complaint with a trained volunteer from the workforce whose role is to listen and help him or her decide what to do. They must explore all possible courses of action the complainant may have, and give him or her the courage to raise the issue with the perpetrator, directly or through a third party, which may in itself settle the matter.

In the words of the European Commission Code of Practice for the Protection of the Dignity of Men and Women at Work, employers are advised to 'designate someone to provide advice and assistance to employees subjected to sexual harassment where possible with responsibilities to assist in the resolution of any problems'. The formality of this role will vary between organisations.

Volunteer	Adviser	Harassment Officer	Professional Counsellor /EAP
informal	informal	formal	formal
untrained	part-trained	trained	trained
amateur	volunteer		

←——————————————————————————————→

In some organisations all these roles will be enacted at varying stages in the procedure.

The informal volunteer, or 'buddy', untrained in any 'professional' sense, will be a colleague possibly, or at least a peer. Organisations are fortunate if they have employees who are willing to help in this way.

The adviser will have more experience and training, and the harassment or equal opportunities officer may be in a formal post which includes not only helping victims, respondents and witnesses but also monitoring, evaluation, training and awareness-raising. The harassment or equal opportunities officer may be a full-time post in larger organisations, or form only part of someone's duties if the organisation is small.

The professional counsellor may be internal to the organisation or, commonly these days, part of an (external) employee assistance programme (EAP).

However informal and voluntary the level of support, it is essential that individuals in this role:

- understand harassment
- are familiar with company procedure
- are familiar with legislation
- are able to give information
- are able to explain options
- are able to help victims to understand that they can do something if they want to, but are not under any pressure to do so
- are able to talk with respondents and witnesses.

Formal stage

- The complainant makes a formal, written complaint identifying the harasser.
- There is a time limit for settlement of complaints. If the complaint is not dealt with swiftly and decisively, the harassment will probably continue.
- The complaint should be acknowledged in writing as soon as possible and the harasser (accused/suspected) given written notification of it at the same time, with full details of the allegations.
- Those involved in the complaint should not talk

openly about it until the investigation is over. In fact, some organisations suspend the accused on full pay for the period of the investigation.

If a standard grievance procedure is used (although this is not recommended), then it is important that there is a means of lodging a complaint with someone other than the supervisor or line manager. When the issue becomes a matter for disciplinary procedures, or is raised at a time when disciplinary procedures are in force for some other reason, then the harassment complaint should take precedence and the disciplinary action be suspended temporarily.

The complaint must be heard quickly by a panel or an independent person, preferably someone outside the department where the parties involved work. The person or panel members should be fully trained in handling these complaints.

- Both parties should be represented.
- The panel must be reasonably satisfied that the incident took place.
- Both parties should be notified in writing when a decision has been reached.
- If the complaint is upheld, then any disciplinary action should be taken as soon as possible.

. . . And afterwards?

Where the resulting action involves separating the parties to the complaint, it is the harasser who should be moved, transferred or suspended, not the complainant.

Even where the complaint is not upheld, there may still be such bad feeling between the parties because of the accusation that some change in their working location or relationship should occur to allow the matter to be forgotten. In all cases everything possible should be done to avoid further harassment and the complainant should be given a written undertaking that he or she will not be victimised or suffer further detriment.

Finally, we should remember that there may be instances where it is a third party who should raise the alarm with respect to bullying and sexual harassment. Surveys show that not only do employees find themselves victims; as many, if not more, find themselves witness to bullying and harassment. It is vital that any third party observer alerts others so that the suspected behaviour can be investigated. Where bullying and sexual harassment have been seen to happen, but the victim will not make a complaint, it might still be possible to counsel the perpetrators with a view to enabling them to see how wrong their actions are. If people can harass one individual, then there is a good chance they may harass others. Investigations prompted by a third party might reveal other current or past victims who could be encouraged to come forward.

Checklist

You must make your staff aware of your procedure, either by giving them individual copies, or by posting a summary in a public place. It should always state:

- how to make the complaint
- how the matter will be investigated
- the timetable for investigation
- employees' rights to representation
- details of the appeals procedure
- the requirement for confidentiality

- whether, and in what circumstances, mediation is available
- the remedial sanctions which may be invoked against the bully or harasser.

Complaints about bullying and sexual harassment can be made by the victim or by a third party.

Procedures should initially be informal, followed by a formal process if necessary.

Informal procedure

- Are there trained volunteers?
- Do employees know where to locate them?
- Do employees know what the volunteer/counsellor will and can do?
- Do employees know that they can bring a complaint about something that they have witnessed or even suspect?

Formal procedure

- There is a formal, written complaint identifying harasser and incident.
- The complaint is acknowledged in writing on receipt (within two working days).
- The alleged harasser is notified in writing, with full details of the allegations (within two working days).
- A full investigation is made by a panel or independent person (within 10 working days).
- The results of the investigation are notified to both parties in writing within three working days of the findings being agreed).
- Any further action is taken as soon as possible.

- The complainant is given a written undertaking that no further victimisation will take place.
- Comprehensive records are kept of the investigation, its findings and subsequent actions.

Employees can also receive advice and support from external agencies such as the Citizens' Advice Bureau, and the issue may end up being referred to some external, probably legal, proceedings. It is always better if these matters can be resolved internally.

How do we conduct an investigation?

- A panel or person begins the procedure.
- Establish initially that the incident did in fact occur.
- Written statements are collected.
- Oral evidence is collected in the presence of the chosen representatives of the parties.
- Decisions are reached.
- The outcome is notified to the parties in writing.
- Recommendations for the next step are made.

How do we conduct the interview?

You will not get a complete picture without interviewing the parties involved. These would normally be:

- complainant/victim
- respondent/harasser
- witnesses.

It may become necessary to use these legalistic terms, but remember this is a sensitive organisational investigation, not a TV courtroom drama.

All the parties must be put at ease and encouraged to understand both the confidentiality and the seriousness of the investigation. They must know who is involved, how the process works and what the outcomes might be. Do everything you can to encourage the individuals to attend accompanied by someone else, as it will help them to relax and give them someone with whom to share reflections later. All of those involved are entitled to have representation – be it a friend or colleague, or a harassment officer or trade union official.

The overall purpose of the interviews is to establish what happened and why, and how the respective parties view the incident; to gather the facts but not to extend the accusations.

Complainant/victim

- Ask what happened.
- Establish the unwelcome extent of the behaviour.
- Establish the nature/role/status of the harasser.
- Establish the duration of the behaviour.
- Establish the extent (does the harasser/respondent treat everyone the same?).
- Get some idea of the emotional/physical state of the complainant.

Harasser/respondent

- Ask what happened.
- Establish his or her perception of his or her own behaviour.

- Establish his or her perception of the complainant's behaviour.
- Get some idea of the emotional/physical state of the respondent.

Witnesses

- Establish their relationship with complainant.
- Establish their relationship with the respondent.
- Establish any concerns over repercussions and retribution from either party.

Monitoring cases and their outcomes

Some examples of possible outcomes are:

- The allegations were unfounded.
- The case is resolved informally, perhaps involving training and counselling for either or both parties.
- The harasser is transferred within the organisation.
- The harasser is dismissed.
- Disciplinary action is taken against the harasser.
- The complainant is transferred.

What happens next?

In many cases a successful resolution can be achieved at the end of informal discussions or a formal investigation. For some organisations facing what may seem to be the impossible or improbable outcome – the two parties working together in harmony again – mediation may be the means to a solution. Some organisations may even consider mediation without moving to any formal investigation, as they feel it will save money and time. It may also save 'face' for those involved, most of whom will be glad of a way out that stops the bullying and harassment. Mediation helps the parties to agree a course of action and a solution, but it must be adapted to the organisation. Mediation has been used in the business world for many years, usually to close a deal – be it sales or compensation – when the two parties can't agree. Its use in employment issues is relatively new, but growing.

How does mediation work?

- The mediator is a facilitator, and manages the process, not the content.
- The purpose is to find a solution, acceptable to both parties, that is voluntary and allows each to retain dignity.
- The process needs a voluntary agreement that all parties will abide by the course of action and the solution agreed.
- The process is without prejudice and all notes must be destroyed when it ends.
- Confidentiality is paramount in both the agreement and in the independent and joint meetings with the parties involved.
- The mediator must have immunity, and cannot be called as a witness.
- The process requires consensual parties; it won't work if people won't compromise.

Who does it?

It is best to have someone from outside the organisation to gain the most objectivity and trust, eg a professional mediator or an independent consultant.

What happens?

Mediation follows a pattern similar to most negotiation processes:

- *preparation* — review of any evidence and, importantly, setting up the correct environment with a room for meetings, and a waiting room for the parties where they will not encounter the 'opposition', tea, coffee, water, tissues, phones

- *opening* — (preferably with both parties present and the individual victim accompanied by friend, colleague or TU representative)
  - introduction of the issues, on paper and without interruption

- *exploration* — at first broad private meetings with separate parties to gauge feelings
  - moving to concerns for the future and the past
  - looking for solutions: 'I just want an apology and to get on with my job'
  - 'I can't work with this person again'
  - trying to find common ground.

At this stage the parties need to think about how they viewed the situation then and now.

- *negotiation* — this may be done with parties separately or together, and seeks common ground
  - the mediator does not judge their

requests, but just works with them
to gain agreement

- *agreement*   • this must be voluntary throughout, otherwise it will break down.

Mediation should take no longer than one day if the parties really want a solution.

Write the mediation procedure into your policy; include methods of monitoring and enforcing agreements; identify the nature of the mediator, who should be external to the organisation, and say how he or she will be trained. Say where meetings will take place and ensure that the facilities are excellent and that the administration runs smoothly – times, dates, details of cases, etc. Finally, elicit union co-operation where necessary.

There is a constant danger that procedures and incidents will excite the mind and generate activity from which, although one case may be settled, nothing is really learned.

All aspects of bullying and sexual harassment must be viewed and evaluated to ensure that everything that can be done has been done; the decision reached was the right one; the actions taken on the basis of that decision were appropriate; and that the procedure is picking up and dealing with all cases. This requires quantitative and qualitative evaluation at various stages, and against both internal and external benchmarks.

Statistical data

Records must be kept of the

- number of cases
- type of cases

- duration of cases
- decisions made
- follow-up mechanisms used.

Even the most simple statistics produced from this monitoring will reveal any trend in the number and type of cases, and should reassure interested parties that they are being dealt with. This can be further conveyed by looking at similar figures from other organisations in your company's sector or of your organisation's size.

Financial data

Analysis of the figures produced will easily lend itself to expression in terms of manpower utilisation, which can then be costed. There may also be costs associated with the solutions – redeployment or relocation at best and, at worst, compensation, industrial tribunal or out-of-court settlements.

This information will be invaluable if you are having to justify to the holder of the purse-strings continued use, or introduction, of policy and procedures.

Surveys and exit interviews

Information showing the presence and extent of bullying and sexual harassment can be gleaned by means other than the analysis of cases. Surveys and exit interviews are also very useful tools in this respect.

Surveys, when carefully designed, can gauge the extent of the problem, the major issues and, if cleverly worded, how strongly employees feel about what should be done. This can be gauged for example on the response to the question

'What did you do about it?' People who feel strongly will make a complaint; those who don't will ignore the matter.

Exit interviews serve as a major vehicle in providing information about the organisation's culture and management, values and practices. Always conducted in confidence, with a person who is not from the work department, these interviews can elicit frank and open comments that

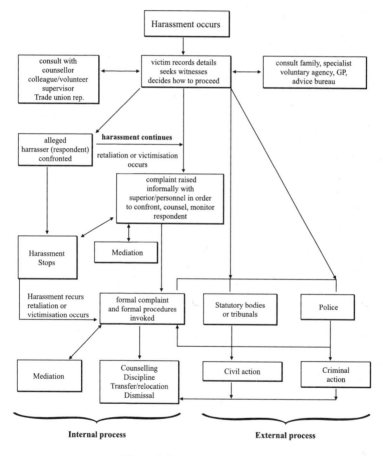

Adapted from Resolving Harassment Complaints
IPD Statement on Harassment at Work

an individual may have been too afraid to bring up during his or her employment.

With all of these monitoring techniques it is important to remember that they should be applied regularly and given prominence at organisational level and publicised to employees. This will encourage good behaviour to continue, and bad (unacceptable) behaviour to stop.

In addition to compiling facts and figures, it is also important to evaluate the way in which investigations are carried out and, in particular, the way the panel operates in evaluating information and reaching its decision. It is a good idea to use past cases as tools for training investigators and panel members, highlighting better ways of working and encouraging best practice. The cases can also be used in general management training and development and for the training of counsellors.

Your target should be to have no cases.

How can I help people enact the policies and procedures?

Awareness-raising

Two main issues arise here:

- Do employees know what bullying and harassment are?
- Does the organisation know the extent of bullying and harassment?

A variety of techniques can be used to raise awareness, including:

- surveys and audits

- leaflets and pamphlets
- posters and signs
- workshops
- confidential helpline
- equality network
- confidential, regular open 'surgery'
- harassment victim advice network
- annual summary of cases provided to the board/JCC
- staff ombudsman
- employee charter
- statement in letters of appointment and contracts of employment
- induction packs and training
- management debriefing
- training
- training!
- training!!

An important aspect of any change in attitude requires everyone in the workforce to understand just what bullying and sexual harassment are. Perceptions vary, but most employers and external bodies would agree that the following descriptors are acceptable. The table also indicates some of the differences between the two, which can be a reason for treating them as separate issues.

Harassment	Workplace bullying
Harassment has a strong physical component, eg contact and touch in all its forms, intrusion into personal space and possessions, damage to possessions including a person's work, etc.	Bullying is primarily psychological (eg criticism) but may become physical later, especially with male bullies, but almost never with female bullies.
Harassment tends to focus on the individual because of what he or she is (eg female, black, disabled, etc).	Anyone will do, especially if they are competent, popular and vulnerable.
Harassment is usually linked to sex, race, prejudice, discrimination, etc.	Sex, race and gender play little or no part; it's usually discrimination on the basis of competence.
Harassment may consist of a single incident, a few incidents or many incidents.	Bullying is rarely restricted to a single incident and tends to be an accumulation of many small incidents.
The person who is being harassed knows almost straight away that he or she is being harassed.	The person being bullied may not realise for weeks or months that he or she is being bullied – until there's a moment of enlightenment.
There is often an element of possession, eg as in stalking.	Phase 1 of bullying is control and subjugation; when this fails, phase 2 is an attempt to 'eliminate' the victim.
Often the harassment is for peer approval, bravado, macho image, etc.	Bullying tends to be secret, behind closed doors with no witnesses.
Harassment takes place both in and out of work.	The bullying takes place largely at work.
The harasser often perceives the victim as easy, albeit sometimes a challenge.	The victim is seen as a threat who must first be controlled and subjugated, and if that doesn't work, 'eliminated'.
The harasser often has specific inadequacies (eg sexual).	The bully is driven by envy and jealousy.
	The bully is inadequate in the area of interpersonal skills.

Adapted from Tim Field's 'Success Unlimited' website

Using surveys

Why?

Many of the organisations claiming to have no bullying or sexual harassment do nothing about trying to discover it. A wise move, you might think: one problem fewer to bother about! As one employer put it, 'We have no company policy relating to this, but this does not mean that I am so naïve as to think bullying does not occur in some instances.'

The 1999 IRS survey found that 'By far the largest single group of employers reporting an increase in bullying in the past two years state that this is due to increasing employee awareness of the issue.' It won't go away, so organisations need to be proactive or when it does emerge it could do as much damage as a tidal wave. If you conduct a survey, you'll be in control and ready to respond.

How?

Questionnaires are the best method. They are short, anonymous and confidential, and you can promise respondents that you will publish a résumé of the findings.

An example of the kind of questions you might ask is given here; under no circumstances should the respondent be encouraged to give actual names at this stage.

- Have you experienced bullying or harassment at work?
- Have you ever been subject to any of the following behaviours and found them to be offensive and unwanted?
    - innuendoes
    - staring

- gestures
- display of pornographic materials
- physical abuse or intimidation
- threat to job security.

What kind of employee exhibited this behaviour?
- a manager?
- a colleague?
- someone who works for you?

- Has a customer or client ever subjected you to unwanted behaviour?
- How often has this happened?
- What did you do about it?

  - Tell someone at work? If so, who?
  - Tell someone at home?
  - Tell the police?
  - Tell your solicitor?

- Did you do anything else?

  - Ignore the behaviour?
  - Make a joke of it?
  - Avoid the person?
  - Ask the person to stop?
  - Report it?
  - Make a complaint?

What then?

When the completed questionnaires have been returned you should:

- analyse the findings
- report them to the organisation

- if instances are reported, be prepared to listen and offer support if individuals wish to come forward
- design, implement and effect policy and procedures to deal with the instances, if you haven't done so already
- be prepared to discover things you don't like
- take it seriously.

The techniques for raising awareness reflect a mix of anonymity and close discussion – from a poster in the canteen to a telephone helpline, to a meeting with a trained counsellor. There should be something appropriate for all employees and all cases. Employees should not have to seek information about what constitutes bullying and sexual harassment, or about what can be done about it. Nor should they be unaware if they are bullying others and of how they can get help.

Counselling

Counselling is recommended at two main stages when dealing with bullying and sexual harassment:

- to enable the victim to establish the extent of his or her case and to stand up to the harasser
- to support both victim and harasser when they return to a 'normal' working relationship. (This is especially important if the case is not proven.)

Counselling is a positive process which can help to protect the individual within an organisation as well as foster a climate of trust and openness.

The counsellor must be:

- respected
- well regarded
- trusted
- credible
- well trained.

The process must enable the:

- issues to be identified and clarified
- reliability and status of reports of the perceived behaviour to be checked out
- victim to overcome fear
- victim to overcome embarrassment
- victim to look for solutions
- victim to manage the situation more effectively
- victim to regain self-esteem
- victim to gain more self-reliance and overcome his or her feeling of helplessness
- victim to obtain support in seeing through his or her decisions and enacting the solutions.

This is achieved by:

- establishing whether the victim would confront the harasser in order to
  - express how that person's behaviour is making him or her feel
  - give a statement of fact
  - be explicit (avoid using euphemisms that might be misunderstood)

- role-play to help the individual rehearse what he or she wants to say

- encouraging the victim to be objective, because he or she may want to make a formal complaint at a later stage
- encouraging the victim to imagine how his or her work environment would change if the bullying and sexual harassment ceased
  - what would be improved
  - what would be the benefit of taking control and changing the circumstances
- considering whether the individual would benefit from assertiveness training
- helping in the evaluation of options
- helping the victim to evaluate in advance his or her reactions if things do not work out as he or she had hoped.

Introducing a counselling service

- Will employees believe that it is there to help?
- Will trade unions support it and see it as impartial?
- Will managers believe it will help them to manage rather than 'mollycoddle' 'weak' staff and foster absenteeism?
- How will it be structured?
- Where will it be located?
- How much will it cost?
- What type of control should there be?
- How will confidentiality be assured?

Training

Recognising and dealing with bullying and sexual harassment are not behaviours that come easily to most people. It is essential that knowledge, skills and attitudes are fostered in the organisation to give employees at all levels the confidence and drive to deal with issues, or indeed prevent them from arising. Different individuals have different learning styles which must be taken into consideration, and different aspects of the subject matter may be better dealt with through different training techniques. Some outline suggestions are given here.

The main groups of people for consideration are:

- individual employees
- supervisors and line managers
- senior managers
- counsellors, professional or 'buddies'
- panel members hearing the case
- personnel department staff.

These cover the complete spectrum of sections or departments in the organisation. The things they need to know about will vary, but will include:

- the policy and procedures
- names, location and function of counsellors and 'buddies'
- recognition of a problem, real or potential
- skills in revealing the problem
- listening skills
- counselling skills

- skills in investigating the problems
- knowledge of legislation and best practice.

The table below indicates what training is needed for key players.

	Policy and procedures	Names, location and function of counsellors	Recognition of real or potential problem	Revealing the problem	Listening	Counselling	Investigation skills	Knowledge of legislation and best practice	What happens next?
Personnel staff	✓✓✓	✓✓✓	✓✓✓	✓✓	✓✓✓	✓✓	✓✓✓	✓✓✓	✓✓✓
Individual employees	✓✓✓	✓✓✓	✓✓✓	✓✓✓				✓	✓
Buddy	✓✓✓	✓✓✓	✓	✓	✓			✓	
Supervisor line managers	✓✓✓	✓✓✓	✓✓✓	✓✓✓	✓✓✓	✓	✓✓	✓✓	✓✓✓
Senior managers	✓✓✓	✓	✓	✓✓	✓✓✓	✓	✓✓	✓✓	✓
Counsellors	✓✓✓	✓✓✓	✓✓✓	✓✓	✓✓✓	✓✓✓		✓	✓
Panel members	✓✓✓	✓	✓✓✓	✓	✓✓✓	✓	✓✓	✓✓✓	✓✓

Showing the depth of knowledge, understanding and skill required.

With this information in mind it will be easy for the organisation to plan and deliver the topic using appropriate methods and working with those who most need the skills and knowledge.

Other sources of training include:

- the TUC, which provides programmes for trade union officials and members

● The Industrial Society, which publishes a pack which includes a book, video and advice on how to develop a training session.

About the techniques

Written: information posters and handbooks: these need to be graphic, to the point, and emphasise what constitutes bullying and sexual harassment.

Seminars and group discussions: these need to be in small groups, discrete and not too lengthy. They should serve to further explore the application of policy and procedures, including how to recognise and reveal instances of harassment and bullying. They may be led by someone with confidence and full knowledge of *all* the range of topics – perhaps a line manager, counsellor or member of the personnel staff.

Case studies: these need to be short and to the point and can be used within the seminar/group discussions session. If they reflect real events, and participants get to know 'what really happened in the end' after they have passed judgement, they will improve people's motivation to listen. If they are too remote from your own business context, you will hear cries of 'That would never happen here.' Again, a well informed trainer/facilitator is needed to guide participants through the case and summarise conclusions.

Role-play: this is something with which most people feel uncomfortable. Case studies are much 'safer'; you have only to give your opinion – you do not have to 'do it'. Nevertheless, we want to encourage certain types of behaviour here and we want participants to know what it feels like to be bullied, to be wrongly accused of sexual harassment, to sit on a panel, or to try to broach the subject with someone whom you feel may be involved.

Participants will feel uneasy and self-conscious, so confidentiality and a very professional trainer/facilitator is required. Twenty-five years of teaching interview skills through role-play has led me to believe that it is the best way to do it, but participants take some persuading. It is better to get it wrong in front of colleagues in a safe situation than to 'blow' a potentially dangerous situation! This role-play should really grow from the comfort and detachment of the case study.

Debriefing

Whenever an instance of harassment or bullying occurs, it should be used as a vehicle for learning. Once the case has been dealt with, and subject to any confidentiality felt necessary, the sharing of the experience will be an invaluable lesson for the future and will give confidence to all involved that they can deal with it. Again, the session should be led by a skilled trainer/facilitator and the manager of the department concerned (provided of course the manager was neither victim nor aggressor). If you can get the victim to contribute, it will help people's understanding. If an individual is found to have been wrongly accused of harassment, it would also be extremely helpful to hear about his or her experience. The more knowledge we have about situations, the better we are able to learn about and deal with them. Training staff to recognise and deal with bullying and harassment should be on-going and should be part of the induction and basic training of all staff. Changes in policy or procedures need to be dealt with as they happen.

In the event that you are fortunate enough to have no 'real' cases, managers should have their knowledge refreshed and polish their skills every 12–18 months. The posters and other publications will keep the information alive for most other employees. There are different training techniques associated with these.

	Written publications eg posters, handbooks	Seminars and discussion groups	Case files, real or fictitious	Role-play	Debriefing
Policy and procedures	✓	✓	✓		
Names, location and function of counsellors	✓				
Problem recognition	✓	✓	✓	✓	✓
Problem revelation	✓	✓	✓	✓	✓
Listening	✓	✓	✓	✓	✓
Counselling	✓	✓	✓	✓	✓
Investigating	✓	✓	✓	✓	✓
Legislation and best practice	✓	✓			✓
What happens next			✓	✓	✓

6

Where does my responsibility end?

☑ The manager has a right to manage
☑ The organisation has a right to control people's behaviour
☑ Employees should look out for themselves
☑ And if the business is thriving?
☑ Finally . . .

As a personnel professional you have several important responsibilities, including contributing to the success of your organisation in achieving business objectives and maintaining the dignity and quality of working life for the people it employs. This is a constantly challenging if unenviable task. How do you know what is acceptable and what is changeable?

The manager has a right to manage

The role of the manager is one of type, trait, contingency, or even a mixture of all three. The manager's job is often fragmented and ill-defined: in many organisations a manager's job description is like a piece of string – as long as it needs to be! Certain generic qualities persist, however, and today's organisation needs managers who are:

- flexible – coping with an ever-changing environment and a broad and sometimes contradictory set of demands
- supportive – acting as coaches and mentors rather than as directors or conductors
- responsive – to customers, other sections of the organisation, peers, colleagues and subordinates
- resilient – constantly regrouping, communicating and persuading others
- visionary – providing leadership, leadership, leadership.

Managers in all organisations must be seen to be performing in certain core activities:

- achieving results
- working through people
- planning and organising
- communicating
- evaluating and monitoring
- getting home occasionally.

The manager has to exercise power to carry out his or her job. Even in organisations that have 'flattened' themselves with the restructuring roller there will still be some who wield power and authority. According to Hofstede (1994) a small power distance, typified by flatter structures, less hierarchy and more matrix management, will reduce the likelihood of harassment. However, in any business the manager's role is to manage and organisations must clarify the limits of power and authority for both the manager and the managed.

The organisation has a right to control people's behaviour

Organisations too are in a privileged position when it comes to exercising power and authority over employees, and they should share the understanding of that position. Organisational culture shapes the behaviour of employees and they, in turn, shape the way the organisation performs. Culture is a soft, holistic concept, also described as

> the psychological assets of an organisation, which can be used to predict what will happen to its financial assets in five years' time.
>
> *Cultures and Organisations*, G. Hofstede, London, HarperCollins, 1994

Culture includes deep-set beliefs about work organisation, authority, reward and control, and it seems that some organisations are just asking for trouble. Should the existing culture be allowed to persist if it breaks the law or treats groups or individuals without respect or dignity or, worse still, with degradation and humiliation?

The armed services, police and fire services are good examples of culture and climate that present major difficulties. These are made worse by the fact that women in non-traditional environments are subject to a higher rate of harassment than women in other areas. Unused to employing women, such organisations do little to prepare for their arrival. Women moving into a previously all-male domain feel isolated and uneasy. Organisations do not change their culture suddenly, and firm and positive steps 'from the top' are now having to be taken. What has taken decades to evolve, and has lasted for further decades, may take decades to change – if it ever does.

The armed forces have a culture where conformity is the norm and accepting different ways of 'doing things around here' does not go comfortably hand in hand with history. The prejudice that has to be overcome by women in these male-dominated cultures is illustrated by the following remarks:

- The Wrens probably suffer sexual harassment. It is what you would expect in a working place with a lot of virile men (Royal Navy Admiral).
- The politically correct creeps behind this ludicrous action are stupid (Royal Navy Admiral).
- The sub-officer referred to her as a 'cow' and told her to get a job in the kitchen (evidence from an industrial tribunal case brought by a female fire-fighter).

The City, it is said, is an example of organisations with a very high level of bullying. Intense pressure, coupled with high numbers of young recruits who lack interpersonal skills and experience of the work environment, lead easily to bullying by older staff with more work experience. It is suggested that an individual's behaviour is perpetuated in a kind of reiterative loop as each group moves up the organisation.

Tim Field describes phenomena that he calls Corporate Bullying or Organisational Bullying. These are characteristic of types of employers who abuse employees with impunity, knowing that the law is weak and jobs are scarce. Typical of such organisations is:

- coercing employees to work 60–80 hours a week on a regular basis, then making life hell for (or dismissing) anyone who objects

- dismissing anyone who looks like having a stress breakdown because it is cheaper to pay unfair dismissal costs than personal injury breakdown claims.
- deeming any employee suffering from stress to be weak and inadequate
- 'encouraging' employees (with promises of promotion and/or threats of disciplinary action) to fabricate complaints about their colleagues.

Employees should look out for themselves

If people in organisations shape the culture, and if a manager's behaviour is strongly influenced by the expectations of peers and subordinates, then 'people power' might be thought sufficient to override possible bullying and sexual harassment. Evidence shows that this is not the case, for several reasons:

- job security may be at risk
- individuals are isolated, believing it is happening only to them
- no one likes confrontation
- victims do not believe they have the right to complain
- they hope it will stop
- they do not know how to complain
- they believe that even if they do complain, nothing will be done.

In environments where bullying is the norm, most people will eventually become either bullies or victims. There may be some bystanders, but most will be sucked in. For the individual it is all about survival; you can either adopt bullying tactics yourself and thus survive by not becoming a victim, or you stand up against bullying and refuse to join in. This latter approach frequently leads to individuals' being bullied, harassed, victimised and scapegoated until they fall ill or leave.

Individuals can cope only if the organisation supports them.

And if the business is thriving?

The order books may be full at the moment, the service demand may be stretching the workforce to capacity, but how long is it going to last? Business today in the public or private sector is a rollercoaster ride. Employees are your most flexible and enduring resource.

If you want to get value for money, value them as human beings and they'll be with you through the downs as well as the ups. If you don't value them, then it won't be long before someone blows the whistle and your business just might not survive.

Finally...

This book asks many questions and suggests some of the answers. The questions are a prompt for you, and your answers will be defined by circumstances as they exist for you. Use the questions to get the answers that are best for you and always keep this thought in mind:

If any behaviour in your organisation results in treating individuals or groups without respect or dignity or, worse still, with degradation and humiliation, then whether it breaks the law or not, it must stop.

Where can I find out more?

Advisory services and publications

Advisory services

Institute of Personnel and Development
IPD House
Camp Road
London
SW19 4UX
Tel.: 020-8971 9000

Industrial Relations Services
18–20 Highbury Place
London
N5 1QP
Tel.: 020-7354 5858

The Industrial Society
Robert Hyde House
48 Bryanston Square
London
W1H 7LN
Tel.: 020-7479 2000

TUC
Congress House
Great Russell Street
London
WC1B 3LS
Tel.: 020-7636 4030

Equal Opportunities Commission
Overseas House
Quay Street
Manchester
M3 3HN
Tel.: 0161-833 9244

Commission for Racial Equality
10–12 Allington Street
London
SW1E 5EH
Tel.: 020-7828 7022

Citizens' Advice Bureau
Myddleton House
115–123 Pentonville Road
London
N1 9LZ
Tel.: 020-7833 2181

International Harassment Network

15 Powis Road
Preston
Lancashire
PR2 1AD
Tel.: 01772 728627

Freedom to Care

PO Box 125
West Molesey
Surrey
KT8 1YE
Voluntary body that encourages organisations
to have a caring attitude.

Women against sexual harassment (WASH)

5th Floor
4 Wild Court
London
WC2B 4AU
Tel.: 020-7405 0430

ACAS

180 Borough High Street
London
SE1 1LW
Tel.: 020-7210 3613
(or local office)

Health and Safety Executive

HSE Information Centre
Broad Lane
Sheffield
S3 7HQ
Tel.: 0114 289 2345

The Suzy Lamplugh Trust
Training Department
PO Box 17818
London
SW14 8WW
Tel.: 020-8876 0305
www.suzylamplugh.org

The Andrea Adams Trust
Maintime House
Basin Road North
Hove
East Sussex
BN41 1WA

The Suzy Lamplugh and Andrea Adams Trusts are providers of assertiveness and self-defence training and advice to employers on making jobs safe from personal attack.

Tim Field's website (www.successunlimited.co.uk) specialises in up-to-date information on bullying.

Publications

ISHMAEL A. *Harassment, Bullying and Violence at Work.* London, Industrial Society, 1999.

Beat Bullying at Work: A guide for trade union representatives and personnel managers. TUC, 1998.

FIELD T. *Bully in Sight.* Success Unlimited, 1996.

Sexual Harassment at Work. TUC guidelines, 1990.

Bullying at Work: The case for reform. MSF, 1998.

No Excuse: Beat bullying at work. London, Industrial Society, 1999 (book, video, training session advice).

'Bullying at work: a survey of 157 employees'. *Employee Health Bulletin.* IRS, April 1999.

'Sexual harassment at work'. *IRS Employment Trends.* September 1996.

RUBENSTEIN M. *Preventing and Remedying Sexual Harassment at Work: A resource manual.* IRS, 1992.

Consider the Cost – Sexual harassment at work. EOC, October 1994.

SUMMERFIELD J. *and* VAN OUDTSHOORN L. *Counselling in the Workplace.* London, Institute of Personnel and Development, 1995.

'Bullying and harassment at work'. *IDS Employment Law Supplement.* May 1996.

IPD Key Fact Sheet: *Harassment at Work.*

Appendix I

Extracts from policies, procedures and training programmes

North Manchester Healthcare NHS Trust
Responsibilities of employees

The Trust's harassment at work policy sets out the responsibilities of employees:

- Inform the harasser they have to stop, or seek advice if they are unable to do so.
- Complain through the proper procedure.
- Treat all colleagues with dignity and respect.
- Ensure that their conduct does not cause offence or misunderstanding.
- Comply with the policy.
- Be encouraged to support colleagues.

(Reproduced from IRS 'Bullying at work: a survey of 157 employers', in *IRS Employee Health Bulletin*, April 1999)

Gloucester City Council

Our promise to combat harassment and bullying

- We will ensure that offices are free from offensive material, graffiti and language.
- We will be patient, polite and respectful in all of our dealings with customers.
- We will give our customers information and clarification in a way that meets their needs.
- We will be as helpful as we can; if we cannot help, we will explain why.
- We will act quickly to put a stop to any incident of harassment or bullying by reinforcing this policy.
- Gloucester City Council will actively promote this policy.

(Reproduced from IRS 'Bullying at work: a survey of 157 employers', in *IRS Employee Health Bulletin*, April 1999)

Bradford Community Health NHS Trust

Code of practice for managers

In adhering to the personal harassment policy of Bradford Community Health NHS Trust, managers must be aware of their responsibilities in order to ensure that the policy is effective.

Dos and don'ts for managers

Do

- Set a good example by treating all staff and customers with dignity and respect
- Be alert to, and correct, unacceptable behaviour
- Ensure staff know how to raise harassment problems
- Deal with any complaints fairly, thoroughly and confidentially, respecting the rights of all parties
- Remember the impact of behaviour determines harassment not the intent.

Don't

- Assume that no complaints means no problems
- Try to dissuade people from making complaints
- Assume that complainants are over sensitive or trouble makers
- Accept 'I didn't mean any harm' as an excuse for harassment
- Allow retaliation or victimisation.

(reproduced from IRS 'Bullying at work: a survey of 157 employers', in *IRS Employee Health Bulletin*, April 1999)

Benefits Agency: General Harassment Officer Training Course

The Benefits Agency has 800 Harassment Officers throughout the UK. There had been Sexual Harassment Officers since 1993. A major review of their role in 1996 concluded that their role should be extended to cover all areas of harassment including bullying. This meant an extensive training programme had to be undertaken to cater for the needs of existing Sexual Harassment Officers to train them in general harassment and to develop a new training course for new Harassment Officers.

A modular four day course was developed for new Harassment Officers and a one day module to complement the existing three day Sexual Harassment Course. All students had to attend a general Equal Opportunities Training course before attending the Harassment Officer Training Course.

Introduction

The course examines harassment and bullying and looks at the new role of Harassment Officers. It is designed for staff who have been newly appointed to the role of Harassment Officer. It can also be used for Personnel Managers/Managers who have management responsibility for Harassment Officers in their business unit.

This course will help participants to improve the way in which they communicate openly, effectively and appropriately in accordance with aspects of the Caring for Staff Core Value and the Business Excellence Framework.

Aims

To provide newly appointed Harassment Officers with the knowledge and skills necessary to carry out their role and to give them the opportunity to practise these skills in a safe environment.

Objectives

At the end of the training event the participants will be able to state and demonstrate the:

- different types of harassment and bullying, how these are recognised and what effect they have on the individual and the organisation
- relevant legislation and Codes of Practice covering harassment and bullying
- limits to the role of Harassment Officer including the boundaries of confidentiality
- processes involved in making a complaint through the Benefits Agency Complaints Procedure and the options available
- relevant skills associated with the role of Harassment Officer

(By kind permission of Ken Frew, BA Equality Team)

Kingston-upon-Hull City Council: Managers' and Supervisors' Personal Harassment Awareness Development

A one-day programme supplemented by written materials including harassment policy and procedures, background to discrimination legislation, and results from previous investigations.

The topics covered are:
What is personal harassment?
Why should managers and supervisors need to know?
The Council's policy and support systems
Legal framework – discrimination and health and safety
The business case
The managers'/Supervisors'/Council's expectations.

The programme also includes the use of video and role-play.

(By kind permission of Dave Dearing – corporate personnel services)

Appendix II

This is from an article in *People Management* reproduced with the kind permission of its author, Olga Aikin.

Sexual harassment

Employers should not wait for a formal complaint to be made before investigating an issue of discrimination. They should act as soon as they have been made aware of it.

In the most recent case on this topic, *Reed and another* v *Stedman* (1999 IDS 634 EAT), Stedman resigned, claiming that her manager's behaviour was unacceptable and that it had damaged her health. The employment tribunal concentrated on four of Stedman's 15 alleged incidents and decided that while these were insufficient individually to amount to harassment, taken together they represented a course of conduct that did amount to harassment and that was a detriment under section 6 of the Sex Discrimination Act 1975.

The tribunal decided not only that the manager was personally liable but that the company was too, because it had failed to investigate his behaviour. Although Stedman had not lodged a grievance or a complaint, the tribunal thought the company had received due notice of her private complaints and deteriorating health. It also felt that the company had breached the duty of mutual trust and confidence.

The Employment Appeals Tribunal upheld the decision and issued guidelines on how employers and claimants should approach sexual harassment claims. It said that:

- sexual harassment consists of words or conduct that are unwelcome to the recipient, that undermine dignity and that create an environment which is hostile and a barrier to sexual equality
- the recipient decides what is acceptable or offensive, and it does not follow that a tribunal should dismiss a complaint if it has a different interpretation of what constitutes acceptable behaviour
- the employment tribunal should not assess individual incidents but should consider all of the circumstances, because the impact of successive incidents may change. For example, something that may not ordinarily bother the victim could appear threatening in the context of earlier behaviour
- some conduct may be inherently unwelcome but, at the other end of the scale, a person might be considered overly sensitive to something that might otherwise be seen as unexceptional behaviour. In such situations, the tribunal must ask whether the person made it clear, by word or conduct, that such behaviour was unwelcome
- it is not necessary for a recipient to make a public fuss – simply walking out of a room might be a sufficient response
- a one-off incident may be harassment and amount to a detriment.

With nearly 100,000 members, the **Institute of Personnel and Development** is the largest organisation in Europe dealing with the management and development of people. The IPD operates its own publishing unit, producing books and research reports for human resource practitioners, students, and general managers charged with people management responsibilities.

Currently there are over 150 titles, covering the full range of personnel and development issues. The books have been commissioned from leading experts in the field and are packed with the latest information and guidance to best practice.

For free copies of the IPD Books Catalogue, please contact the publishing department:

Tel.: 0181-263 3387
Fax: 0181-263 3850
E-mail: *publish@ipd.co.uk*
Web: *www.ipd.co.uk*

Orders for books should be sent direct to:

Plymbridge Distributors
Estover
Plymouth
Devon
PL6 7PZ

Credit card orders:
Tel.: 01752 202 301
Fax: 01752 202 333